CAMILLE SAINT-SAËNS

HAVANAISE

for Violin and Orchestra
Op. 83

Edited by/Herausgegeben von
Wolfgang Birtel

Ernst Eulenburg Ltd

London · Mainz · Madrid · New York · Paris · Prague · Tokyo · Toronto · Zürich

CONTENTS

Preface III

Vorwort V

Prèface VII

Havanaise 1

Ernst Eulenburg Ltd
48 Great Marlborough Street
London W1F 7BB

PREFACE

'Nobody knows more about music all over the world than Monsieur Saint-Saëns', said Claude Debussy in praise of his fellow composer. There can be few, one might add, who have left behind such an extensive body of work, representing every musical genre: Camille Saint-Saëns (1835–1921) composed symphonic and dramatic music, vocal and chamber music, piano, military and ballet music – and, with *L'Assassinat du Duc de Guise* in 1908, the first original film music.

This French musician favoured the violin repertoire in particular with two sonatas, three concertos and a series of smaller works with piano or orchestral accompaniment. Some of the inspiration for these doubtless came from his friendship with the Spanish violinist Pablo de Sarasate, who delighted audiences with his circus tricks and his sweetly languishing tone on the violin. Sarasate gave Saint-Saëns many tips as to what was technically possible on the violin – and the composer dedicated his third violin concerto and the *Rondo Capriccioso* to him. It is without doubt also from his acquaint-

ance with Sarasate that the composer acquired a fondness for Spanish tone colour and folk tunes, most clearly felt in the *Introduction et Rondo capriccioso* Opus 28, in the *Havanaise* Opus 83 and in the *Caprice andalou* Opus 122.

In November 1885 Camille Saint-Saëns set off on a concert tour with the Cuban violinist Diaz Albertini, travelling through northern France on the way to Germany. On a cold wet evening, the crackling of a fire in the hearth of a desolate hotel is said to have inspired him to write a melody that he incorporated in his *Havanaise* two years later. Indeed, he dedicated this composition to Albertini, his companion on the tour. It was published in 1888; the composer also orchestrated the original piano accompaniment.

In the *Habanera*, a Spanish dance of Cuban origin, the composer lets the violin wallow in captivating melodies while also giving the performer plenty of opportunity for a virtuoso display of dazzling technique – an effective bravura piece.

Wolfgang Birtel
Translation: Julia Rushworth

VORWORT

„Niemand kennt die Musik der ganzen Welt besser als Monsieur Saint-Saëns", lobte Claude Debussy seinen Komponistenkollegen, und nur wenige, darf man hinzufügen, haben ein derartig umfangreiches und alle Gattungen abdeckendes Gesamtwerk hinterlassen wie er: Symphonische und dramatische Musik, Vokal- und Kammermusik, Klavier-, Militär- und Ballettmusik hat Camille Saint-Saëns (1835–1921) komponiert, aber auch mit *L'Assassinat du Duc de Guise* 1908 die erste originale Filmmusik geliefert.

Das Geigenrepertoire hat der französische Musiker dabei besonders bedacht: mit zwei Sonaten, drei Konzerten und einer Reihe kleinerer Werke mit Klavier- oder Orchesterbegleitung. Dazu hat sicher auch die Freundschaft mit dem spanischen Geiger Pablo de Sarasate beigetragen, der das Publikum mit seinen zirzensischen Kunststücken und seinem süß-schmachtenden Ton auf der Violine verzückte. Er gab Saint-Saëns so manchen Tipp, was auf der Geige technisch möglich ist – ihm widmete er auch sein drittes Violinkonzert und das *Rondo capriccioso*. Sicherlich rührt von der Bekanntschaft mit dem Geiger auch des Komponisten Faible für spanisches Kolorit, für die Folklore des Nachbarlandes her, das am deutlichsten in *Introduction et Rondo capriccioso*, opus 28, in der *Havanaise*, opus 83, und in der *Caprice andalou*, opus 122, zu spüren ist.

Im November 1885 startete Camille Saint-Saëns mit dem kubanischen Geiger Diaz Albertini zu einer Konzerttournee, die ihn auf der Durchreise nach Deutschland in den Norden Frankreichs führte. An einem nasskalten Abend soll ihn das Knistern eines Kaminfeuers in einem trostlosen Hotel zu einem melodischen Einfall inspiriert haben, den er zwei Jahre später in seine *Havanaise* einbaute. Die Komposition widmete er übrigens seinem Tourgefährten Albertini. Sie erschien 1888 im Druck; den originalen Klavierpart orchestrierte der Komponist auch.

In der *Habanera*, einem spanischen Tanz kubanischer Herkunft, lässt der Komponist die Violine mit einschmeichelnden Melodien schwelgen, gibt den Interpreten aber auch reichlich Gelegenheit zu technisch virtuosem Feuerwerk – ein effektvolles Bravourstück.

Wolfgang Birtel

PRÉFACE

« Saint-Saëns est l'homme qui sait le mieux la musique du monde entier ». C'est par ces mots que Claude Debussy faisait l'éloge de son homologue. Et, faudrait-il ajouter, bien peu de compositeurs ont laissé un œuvre aussi nombreux, couvrant tous les genres : Camille Saint-Saëns (1835–1921) a composé des musiques symphoniques et dramatiques, vocales et de chambre, pour piano, militaires, de ballet – mais aussi, avec *L'Assassinat du Duc de Guise* en 1908, la première musique de film originale.

Ce faisant, le musicien français a accordé une place toute particulière au répertoire du violon : avec deux sonates, trois concertos et une série de petites œuvres avec accompagnement de piano et d'orchestre. L'amitié qui le liait au violoniste espagnol Pablo de Sarasate, qui enchantait le public par ses tours de cirque et le ton langoureux de guimauve qu'il tirait de son violon, a sans nul doute contribué également à cet intérêt. Il donna maints conseils à Saint-Saëns quant aux possibilités techniques du violon – c'est à lui que celui-ci dédia son troisième concerto pour violon et son *Rondo capriccioso*. Cette relation personnelle avec le violoniste explique certainement aussi le faible du compositeur pour le coloris et le folklore espagnols, qui se manifeste le plus nettement dans *l'Introduction et Rondo capriccioso*, opus 28, la *Havanaise*, opus 83, et le *Caprice andalou*, opus 122.

En novembre 1885, Camille Saint-Saëns entama avec le violoniste cubain Diaz Albertini une tournée de concert qui le mena en Allemagne en passant par le nord de la France. Par un soir bruineux et froid, le crépitement du feu dans la cheminée d'un hôtel déprimant lui aurait inspiré une mélodie qu'il intégra deux ans plus tard à sa *Havanaise* – composition qu'il dédia d'ailleurs à son compagnon de tournée Albertini. Elle fut publiée en 1888 ; le compositeur orchestra également la partie pour piano originale.

Dans la *Havanaise*, danse espagnole d'origine cubaine, le compositeur fait s'enivrer le violon de mélodies enjôleuses, mais donne aussi largement à l'interprète l'occasion de se livrer à un feu d'artifice d'une grande virtuosité technique – un morceau de bravoure spectaculaire.

Wolfgang Birtel
Traduction : Martine Paulauskas

HAVANAISE

Camille Saint-Saëns
(1835–1921)
op. 83

Edited by Wolfgang Birtel
© 2015 Ernst Eulenburg Ltd, London
and Ernst Eulenburg & Co GmbH, Mainz

9

14

18

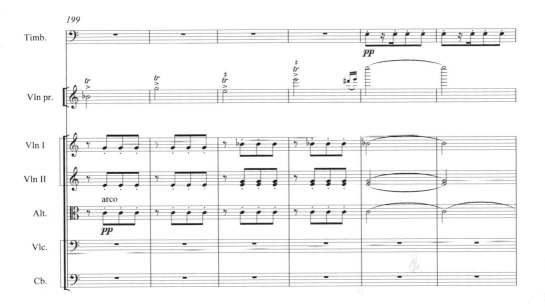

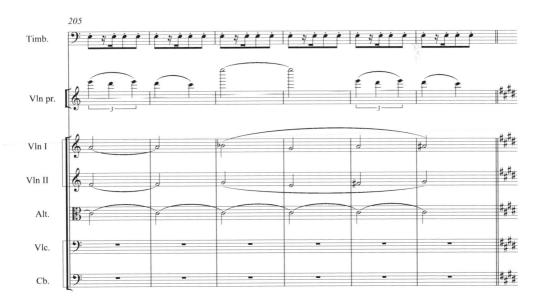

22

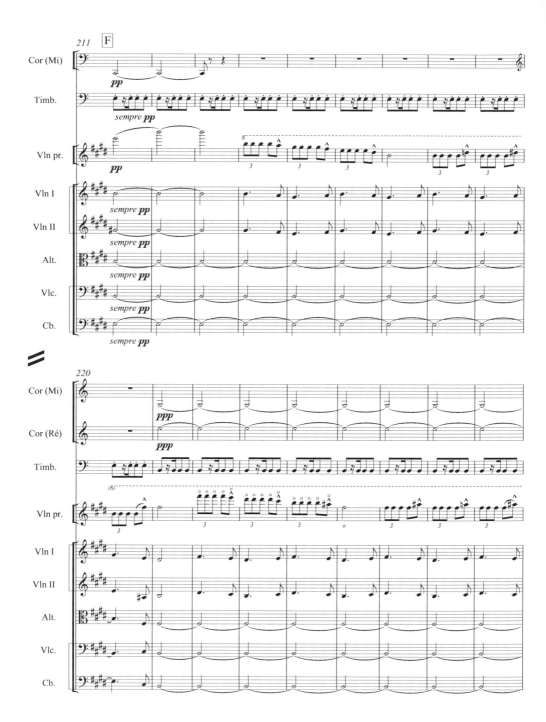

28

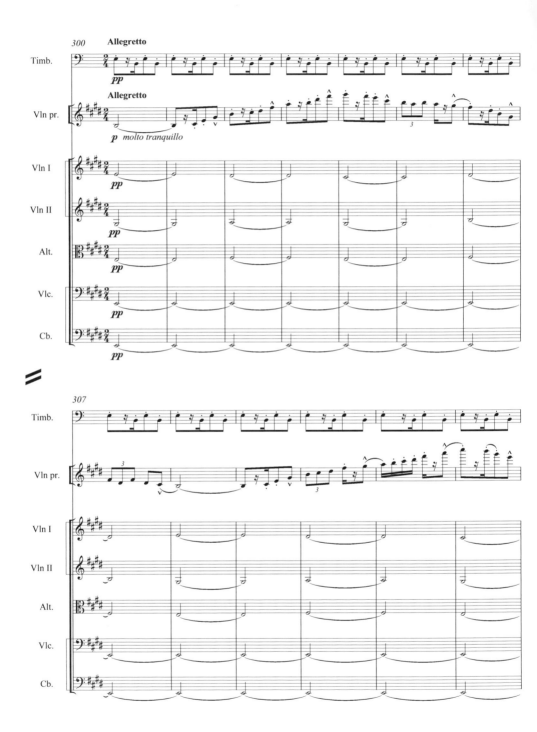